THE

GHOST

IN THE

MACHINE

POEMS BY BARBARA LENNOX

ISBN: 979-8-70265592-5

DEDICATION

To my late parents, who gave me that greatest of gifts, a love of reading.

TABLE OF CONTENTS

TABLE OF CONTENTS (CONTINUED)

TABLE OF CONTENTS (CONTINUED)

THE GHOST IN THE MACHINE

Listen, as I speak to you in dead languages.
Hear me in the roar of the solar wind,
the beat of an owl's wing,
the song of the dodo.

You may search, but never find me;
I am no spike of frequency,
no trail in a bubble chamber,
no cat in a box.

I'm an equation without a solution,
a hypothesis that can never be proved,
the square root of minus one.
I'm the seventh quark, the seventh seal,
the answer to everything.

I am not life or death
but the smoke of their collision,
the first breath, the last gasp.
I'm neither faith nor reason,
but the shadow of a doubt.

I'm the journey, not the arrival,
the search, and not the finding.
I am nowhere and everywhere,
nothing and everything.

I am always.

INTRODUCTION

These poems were written over a 20 year period. Some have appeared in anthologies and exhibitions, details of which can be found in the Appendix. Many appeared in a single-author collection *The Dark Side of the Moon*, published in 2010 by *WomenWord Books*. Some of these particular poems have been amended and updated for inclusion in this collection.

The poems have been inspired by a huge range of topics. As a lover of the outdoors, particularly of Scotland, many of my poems explore aspects of nature, and so there are poems about birds, animals, plants, places and the seasons of the year. My fascination with Scottish history and mythology has also worked its way into my poetry. As a former scientist, I'm interested in ideas in general and scientific ideas in particular, and many of them have found their way into my poems. Above all, the obsession of any human with love, loss, life, death, and all aspects of the human condition, has been the driver for much of my poetry.

I hope you enjoy reading the poems. I certainly enjoyed writing them. Further information about individual poems can be found in the Notes.

NATURE

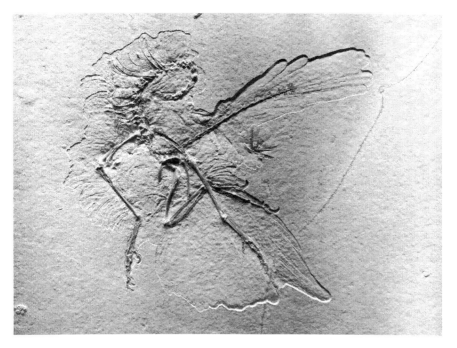

They've cracked you from the rock,
as once you broke from the shell . . .

ARCHEOPTERYX

This stone speaks
of how you met your death –
a smothering of ash and silt,
one last cry crushed by the years,
to silence.

Your body is a fault-line now,
an epitaph of runic bones,
a long slow settling in the grave,
smeared to a layer of limestone.

Now they've cracked you from the rock,
as once you broke from the shell.
Quarried from your tomb,
you have been born again,
to tell the story of yourself.

Your arched bones speak.
Raised ribs of rock
take flesh and form.
A trace of feathers whispers your name.

OWL

She shears the night's wind,
seine-nets her senses to harvest
every sound and movement.
She is snowfall in a summer's dusk.

Nothing escapes her notice;
no twitch of a whisker,
no cheep from a nest,
no leaf-litter rustle.

Ears inhale every sound,
eyes every single photon.
Meshed feathers silence the air
as she cups the wind,
feet outstretched in the fall.

Her cry is answered,
a scream cut off,
a small death in the dark.

PEREGRINE

He came, walking down her quiet meadows,
through the dry grasses where careless sparrows
scatter themselves from the cottonwood trees.
He seemed to be content, a man at ease
with himself and the world. How was it then
she knew that lack in him? He was huntsman
to her doe-like desire not to be seen,
bondsman to her wish to hold him as a queen
holds her subjects, to fill that empty space
she sensed had her shape. But how to outpace
the wind? How to hold a falcon earthbound?
A fish to the shore? Better to be drowned
herself than keep him tethered, wild thing
that he was. And so, in the end, smiling,
she let him leave. She let him fly away.
And, later, there was nothing to outweigh
the gap he left, the space that had his shape.
Her heart had no map for this, no landscape
for loss and longing, no balm for duty
amongst the trees and grasses, nor safety
from regret for the hand setting him loose
to hunt his world. And now, what is the use
of living like this? She is prisoner
of her hard gift of freedom, wanderer
in her unquiet meadows. And there she stands,
a barred hawk's feather in her empty hands.

OYSTERCATCHERS

They're commoner now.
Since the crash you see them
flocking together, demanding their rights.
'Me, me, me!'
But these sharp-suited opportunists
have come down in the world.
See those bloodshot eyes?
That's from slumming it with the hoi polloi,
grubbing for existence, turning over rocks
to see what crawls out. They're forced to live
on a diet of worms when what they crave
is the salt slip of shellfish.
But there's not an oyster to be had.
'Not a single f***ing oyster!'

HAWKING

She's at her hunting weight –
two pounds, two ounces
of feather, beak and bone,
a bag of sugar's weight
perched on my fist.
And yet she's light,
ready for the off,
half-poised for flight.

I grip her jesses as a child
tethers a balloon
and feel the same lift,
the urge of air under the wing,
the wrack and tilt of the ground,
the hurtling plummet,
the wind's rasp.

I feel the skull crack in my grip,
but is my cry hers or the hares?
Is the thread of blood on my lip
sweet or sour?

BROCK

You know them
by the mess they
leave – grubbed
scrapes, scat,
a certain stench.
They are navvies
working the night,
diggers of setts
at dawn and dusk,
hunters of worms
and hedgehogs.
They are sleek
and powerful
under the moon,
with limbs like shovels.
They are striped with midnight.

HORSES

Where have they gone, the horses,
the wild-eyed stallions, the steady cobs,
the duns, the bays, the chestnuts?
Where are the high-steppers,
the big-footed drays,
the mild-mannered mares
and flighty fillies?
Where are the herds that ran
and thundered, manes flying, hooves
churning, high-hearted, racing the wind?

Now there's a silence from the steppes,
the breeding grounds, the parks,
the paddocks, and the bruised battlefields.
Where have they gone, the horses?

But if you listen, beneath the traffic,
you'll hear an echo of clopping hooves,
and, in the fields, the straight drill of the land
is pocked with hoof-prints.
You can smell their sweat, their saddle-leather,
and taste the red-coated, silver-horned morning.

Feel warm damp velvet lipping your palm,
their breath, slow and solemn,
on the back of your mind.
And think of Pegasus wings flying, flying . . .

SNOWDROPS

I have grown used to winter,
to the inconveniences of snow,
to shrivelled days and skies of stars
gripped in the night's black ice.
I am no longer surprised by rime
on the grass, the bones of trees
edging the bleak fields,
that hoar-frost gleam in the north.

But in the woods there is a drift of white
that is no winter's relic,
no thaw of ice among the clenched
leaves of last year's autumn.
For this snow lingers, blossoming,
and does not yield to the warmth
of a gloved hand. These milk-pale bells
ring out their quiet carillon
and seem to summon the days
to breathe once more, the fingers
of winter's fist to uncurl and ease apart.

WOOLLY WILLOW

You think it strange to find me here
on the heights, in wind and cloud,
in bitter winter weather.

My cousins, down in the valley,
root themselves in wet tilth,
lift green heads to the sky,
trail their tresses in flowing streams,
lay their fingers on the face of the waters.

Here among the screes, in granite gravel,
there's little of the moisture my sort crave.
It condenses and falls but trickles away,
strains itself through bedrock,
is torn away by wind, stripped
by searing summer light.

I'm forced to cling to the earth
and thrust my roots down into rock
until I barely have the strength to lift my head
above the parapet.

Small wonder I've turned stunted and ugly.
No pre-Raphaelite willow, me.
But I can dream. I can still dream.

WINTER I

It comes from the North,
banners beating the wind,
grey smoke pluming the sky,
a legion on the edge of sight,
silent as wolves.
The battlements of hills have fallen.
They glitter with weapons now –
quivers of ice and silver sabres –
and we have flown the white flag.

Our colours have fled,
red and green and autumn gold.
They've turned their heels
and headed for the South.
Only we remain, blazoned in black,
to etch the annals of this year's war
on the fields' white pages.

For a time the world will lie
like a cold pearl in a grey shell of sky,
while we endure, waiting for the siege to lift,
for the armies to retreat, slip North by night
through high passes in the hills.

They are heading for their lairs of stone,
leaving in their wake small deaths –
shrubs and sparrows and shoots
shrivelled by the wind.
But they leave their own dead too –
a pale drift pierced by reeds,
a wing of snow slumped beneath a northern slope,
a spate of water bleeding to the sea.

WINTER II

It begins quietly:
a drawing in at the edges,
a shrinkage of light,
a shiver in the air,
then a month-long
frenzy of denial.

Old traditions are unearthed
from the attic, dusted off,
put up. But celebrations
ring hollow as bells toll
the shrunken days
and fail to drive back the dark.

Days pass, drear weeks,
until there seems no end to it.
But breathe in and hold your breath
because it *will* end. Have faith
until all you're left with is hope.

That's what it's waiting for.
That's when it will slip away.

TEMPERATURE INVERSION

A day in February, after a night of frost,
and I walked the ice-feathered track,
my breath eider-downing the day.
Even the sun was frozen,
cold as brass in a pewter sky,
etched by vapours and thin skeins of geese.

Breathing was easy then, limbs and muscles loose,
and I thought of little as I climbed through heather.
Only of the walk, the cold, the summit.

I could have stayed forever there,
laved in sunlight, drinking the day.
I could have built a house of stone and moss,
slaked my thirst with cold clear light,
fed on heather-tips and crowberries,
made my home with shy blue hares.

Instead, facing the sun, I descended late,
down fans of scree, through ice-bound streams,
into vapour, clouds and darkness.
Then one last gift, one brief moment;
cloud was ripped by a saw-tooth of pines
to let the moon shine through, marbling the night.
As now, at the end of the ward,
someone turns on a lamp.

Breathing is not easy here,
summits long since out of reach,
and darkness gasps and falters
by my snow-bound winter bed.
Saline drips melt-water under the ice,
vapour trails across a pewter screen,
and bird skeins vanish as the moon-lamp fades
to fog and frost and nightfall.

SUMMERS

Summers were endless once,
months of sun and sandwiches,
and sprinklers on the lawn,
steak pie al fresco, and mystery tours
that went to places as mysterious
as Pittenweem or Crail.

It was no holiday, summer,
just a different regime.
We children had our work to do:
peas to pick, rasps to harvest,
carrots to weed.
Summer was no picnic.

Even the picnics were no picnic
in those days:
orange smiles in glass bottles,
milky tea in flasks for grownups,
sandwiches of pan loaf slices –
cheese or egg or lettuce.
'Eat them up;
I didn't carry them all this way for nothing.'

like the rest of the stuff:
windbreaks and suntan cream,
buckets and spades and plastic balls,
swimming suits in ruched cotton,
towels and tubes of stuff for midges.

The tide was always out in those days,
and we crossed razor-shell sharp sand
in a gale of wind, racing for the waves.
The sea was warm at first, on feet and ankles,
then chilled the knees and thighs,
and froze the parts we had no name for.
Greatly daring, we screamed into the sea,
crouched to our necks, rubber-ringed for safety.

'It's warmer if you have a pee',
said Tracy Buist, from the housing estate.
So we tried it and it was.

Summers were endless once.

November

Tonight we lit a fire in the garden,
in the brambled waste beyond the trees.
All evening we have fed the flames
with gathered wood, old chairs, prunings,
and the bleached stems of lovage.

Sparks lift and spiral on the wind
as we light our fireworks –
goblin showers, dragons' breath,
fairy fountains.
They leave a taste of smoke on the lips,
and old gods in the blood.

Dark seeps from shadow
and fire ebbs away to ash.
The night stoops down,
crooning on the wind,
as we stamp our feet
against the cold and dark,
against the passing of things.

Then one last gleam
slides on up-tossed antlers,
on the spear's red edge,
and we are chanting, chanting,
chanting.

LOW SPRINGS

Twice a day, the miracle
of transmutation. Water turns to mud,
to beach, to bank.
It seems less a falling away
than a rising up of continents.

There are rivers here with no name,
high ground, unsurmounted,
the bones of ships exposed to the sky.
Lost villages ring with barnacled bells,
home now to razor-shells, sea-urchins,
brittle stars.

For a time this hidden land
steams in the sun, an exhalation
and a holding of breath.
Then it's subsumed once more;
mud trickles away, rivers merge,
banks shrink and slip beneath
a ripple of sunlight.

It's quiet now, down in the dark,
in the tug of the tide,
where stars pick their way through sand,
and kelp undulates like serpents.

BEN NEVIS

It lies behind your mind,
massive and majestic.
You've seen it by morning,
by moonlight, and not seen it
more often than not.
Yet still it's there, behind the mist,
behind the clouds, in torrents of snow
or troubled waters.

You travel it with your eyes,
terrify yourself with contours,
map its ways and almost feel it
hard beneath your feet.

Yet even there in distance,
in the clarity of winter,
or summer dawn or autumn noon,
you see it sometimes,
lying behind those nearer peaks –
a bulwark on the edge of sight,
massive and magnetic,
pulling you north or south,
drawing the eye, the heart.

ROUNDING THE HORN

It's all hands on deck in the dog watch,
with the wind gusting and the long night falling.
We're as south as a man can sail,
running down the easting out of Adelaide,
on a broad reach in a half-gale,
with a cargo of tea and silk and opium.

But now we've turned our stern to the wind
and there's nothing behind, nothing ahead,
but a scream of wind and roiling ocean.
To the north looms land and ship-killing waters,
to the south a shifting continent of ice.
Fathoms deep below lie cold whale waters.

Night falls but light lingers
in the eldritch gleam of sea-ice
and the rush of phosphorescence
in roaring breakers. Above, stars glitter,
cold and clear and careless.
Below, a flame flickers in the binnacle.

We are little more than glimmers of life,
nothing more than frail barques
on a black, black ocean.

CLIMBING THE LINE

Stand at the foot of the face.
Lay palm upon rock
and merge yourself with granite.
This stone is unforgiving of softness,
yet it must have its weakness.
So search out the tilt and thrust
of a molten folding together
to find the line to travel.

Your strength is of a different order –
swifter, transient – your movement
from one point of balance to the next.
You are muscles burning, palms sweating.
You are the terror of the fall.

You must forget you're gravity's victim
and turn your thoughts to stone,
your will to steel. Become the dancer
and the dance. Become life on the edge,
life on the line, a fly on a wall.

Hold yourself by wire and webbing,
by nut and bolt, by the rip stop
of a fingerprint's grip.
Reach from crack to crevice,
from hold to ledge.
Strain through that crux
of empty overhanging air.

Measure time by heartbeats,
by the shift of shadows,
the slide of sun on your back.
Measure distance by the length
of your own reaching body.

Gauge success by the change in angle,
the respite of a third dimension.
Know then you've climbed the line
of your mind's eye.

MUNRO-BAGGING

I look across the layers of land
and search for peaks
that brush against the sky.
It marks them out as summits
to be claimed and numbered.

One group there, linked by a ridge,
others clustered around a loch,
another still remote and trackless.
But I will plan my route
and win that distant goal –
some shapeless hill whose name
means peak of the rock
or some such thing.
I know its name as eighty four,
a blank space to be ticked
and squirreled away.

In time I'll leave that cairned and cloudy peak
Head for number eighty five,
another ill-formed mound of stone.

Yet one day, months or years from now,
I will recall that peak,
not as a number but as a field of scree,
a wing of snow, a route through heather
and sweet wild gale,
the smell of sunrise and of sweat,
the rasp of air, a bone-deep ache,

and the taste of an old, old name on my tongue.

THE FOREST

Step between these trees
and you step into a church.
Here light is filtered through stained leaves,
scythed by the shadows
of barked columns.

Above you curves a vault
of branches, cross-ribbed with larch
and finialled with pine. Walk into this nave
of woodland and it will open out
to chapels of birch, transepts of aspen.
Breathe in the incense of fern
and moss and reed.

High up, in the clerestory of treetops,
you will hear the choir –
the soprano solo of a thrush
above the organ bass of wind.

There ought to be an altar here
in this insect haze of light.
But it's not that stone,
that fallen oak, that unexplained mound.

It's all around you, beneath and above.
It was here before you were born,
will be here long after.
It's older than these birds,
those trees, this wood, that wind.

MOORLAND IN RAIN

All day it rained and we, at the edge of the moors,
watched the gutters fill, the brook darken with peat.
All that day we heard the sound of trickling,
the beat and flurry, the dull hiss and steady drip until,
tiring of the rain, we left our inn for the world of water.

All evening, facing the wind, we walked the margins of the
    clouds.
There, on the moor, pools purled and spawn glistened.
All that evening, in the rush and plume of the air,
we held thunderheads in our cold wet hands while, far below,
in the cleft of a valley, our inn lay crouched.

All night the rain lashed the window,
as we, in our quiet bed, breathed in the sweet wild gale.
All that night we held each other and dreamed,
of moorland and rainclouds, granite and slate,
of stratus and nimbus and cirrus.

ISLAND I

I crossed by ferry to the far island,
and left my mainland self behind.

Water lies between my present and my past,
the salty amnion of separation,
and I have become an island creature,
dweller on the margins of an old ocean.

Life is liminal on this upwelling of rock,
its harvests bog-cotton and cloud,
its gleanings the leavings of a frugal sea.
But life persists, here in this singularity.

It lingers like the last of the light
that washes black basalt to silver
and draws the horizon closer than my own heart,
as illusory and numinous as any island.

ISLAND II

This is a place of distance,
a land that layers itself.
Headlands plunge to necks of water,
surge upwards in a mass of slopes.

Behind each tongue of land
lies yet another, curved and ridged,
and there, at the edge of sight,
a single shaded contour
that could be cloud or mountain,
or both.

This is a place of water,
of firths and sounds and narrow channels,
of fretted waves and breathing swells.
From every slope there rings
a rush and purl of streams
pocked by peat-dark tarns.

This is a place of sky,
of coiling clouds that haze the hills.
High cirrus plumes its feathers
in a plane of air and wind.
And, from the West, a shadow slants,
rain shot through with sun.

Above all, this is a place of light,
a glittering on calm water,
a glint of turning breakers,
a wash that paints the hills
to bracken-green and ochre.

Dawn is the colour of a dove's breast,
noon a cerulean blue and, at dusk,
a golden haze layers itself in distance,
reflected by water, filtered by sky,
the luminous light of the West.

River

Hold me up to the sky
and light falls through me.
Hold me in your hands
and I slip between your fingers.
Who'd think I could carve mountains,
smooth coasts to plains,
change the face of the earth?

I began as cloud in an upland hollow,
rain sifting across the hills,
a patch of snow melting in the April sun.
I have been water in all its forms.

But now I'm in gravity's grasp.
so down I go, seeping and sliding.
I gurgle and giggle, bubble and babble,
I purl and lap and lip and dribble.
I gather and grow, grumble and growl.

I grind rocks in a slobber of foam,
break through fault lines and
throw myself from clifftops
to punch the fist of my falling
down into bedrock.

But now I've turned silent
as I slip my way past alder woods
and reed banks, through deep lochs
that nurse ancient creatures.
I slither through water-meadows
muddied by the hoof-prints of ox bows.

In time, I'll taste salt on my lips
and I'll grow gravid with the tide.
I'll broaden and slow,
let slip my burden of silt
to abandon all I hold of the land,
and leave it altered behind me.

Ahead is a sword sharp horizon, a rising moon.
I rush to meet it.

THE PAST

We broke the light with our bold wings,
like eagles on a thermal . . .

DAEDALUS

In the end, we fled from Knossos, leaving behind a labyrinth,
a monster, and the wrath and envy of Kings.
I had grown great by then, half-artificer, half-magician,
with a son to follow me, to go further than I,
to bend the world, even the Gods' own will.

But not meanly did we flee those little men,
not in shadows or by night, but in sunlight on a fair morning,
lifting into the air. For I had bound feathers with wax,
pinioned and primaried to ride the wind,
to breast the unfolding light, flexing into ardent skies.

And how we flew, Icarus and I! How we bent the air!
We broke the light with our bold wings,
like eagles on a thermal, rising into the day.
And there I lingered, the earth turning beneath me,
lit by the moons of upturned faces, gaping with awe.

But my son sought the fire of Phaeton's carriage.
Bright spirit, drawn to a brighter, he crested the clouds.
And so he fell, on a stream of wax and charred feathers.
Too close, too far, too ambitious. The sin was mine,
although he went further than I. But the death was his.

ORB-WEAVER

I am three fates in one:
Spinner, Weaver, Shearer of the thread.
There's death in my filigree
flutterings, as I net the wind
and loom a winding sheet
to shroud my sweet sarcophagi.

I'm Penelope of the orchard,
Arachne of the outhouse,
and you may see me there
in the goose-month, nerve-centre
of a plexus of silk and dew,
grave-cloths and lace.

When winter comes, I'll vanish,
curl myself to a gleam of facets
in the cracks of the world.
I'm the black widow of shadows
where I shuttle out the dark:
Clotho, Lachesis, Atropos.

DRYAD

I am become a shepherdess of trees.
I know each by name, by quality:
the strong heart of the pine,
the lax drift of the larch,
the birch, blanching the dusk.
Here, high on our hill, my flock and I
brace ourselves against the storm.

One day, a tree-ring's width from now,
I'll take my stand among them,
my flock, my kin, my sister-brothers.
I'll sink my feet deep in a tilth of needles,
and, twigs and nests in my hair,
raise my arms to gather in the gale,
then gild myself in the brazen blare of sunset.

I'll turn my back on river and sea,
the reek of field and road,
the feel of skin touching skin.
Instead I'll choose the sough of wind,
the hiss of rain, the slow tilt of the world.
I'll feel myself scale over, my limbs branch.
My heartbeat will slow to a viscid flow of sap.

I'll feel my death distance itself.

WAITING FOR RAGNAROK

I am taloned to this spire
of slate and psalms and promises,
pinioned to a compass-wheel of winds,
and I have grown dull, tarnished by time,
gilded only by the breaking light
that rises eastward, where ships,
close-hauled, feather their sails
to match my inclination.

Yet who looks skyward now?
Who is caught by a glint of gold,
the pluck of myth in the heart-strings?
Who remembers what I once was?
I, who gnawed the world's tree roots,
encircled battlements of cloud,
was appeased by the flesh of virgins.
I, who was puissant, rampant,
symbol of dynasties, and western lands
lost to the sea-wolves rampage.

But I am diminished now,
fettered to this crag, this foothill of the sky,
a conflagration cooled by the breeze to bronze,
while my kinfolk languish.
Were-worms and fierce drakes of fire
lie cavern-bound in basalt,
drugged by lava and the reek of gold.

And, oh, how I long for the end,
the lift of storm in the wings,
the beat of Thor's hammer,
the cry of ravens and the wild hunt riding!

And so I strain for the west,
the flame of the falling sun,
the memory of phoenix-breath,
the ache of fire in my jaws.

But I must be patient, fulcrum-poised,
as I turn through air and time,
waiting, through each circling year,
for Ragnarok.

YGGDRASIL

I hold up the whole world,
am a perch for ravens,
an ancient eagle and four wild stags.
A God has hung from my crown,
and I have seen with his given eye.

I rake the rasped wind
with black and brittle nails.
A toss of my head
is a tempest of troubles.
My trunk cannot be girdled.

I am fed with the dews
of the four wells of Midgard.
None knows how far my roots run.
I lay seven-fingered hands
on the face of the waters.

Ravens' tree they name me,
and Gallows tree.
My keys unlock the wide woods
and the wild waysides.
I scatter my seeds to the storm.

I have made spears and shield-rims,
ship-oars and wheel-spokes,
gateways and gunwales.
I have been the wings of birds
riding the winds of war.

Will you grieve at my going?
When I'm bones in the greenwood,
black twigs in the graveyard,
and gaps in the hedgerows?
When I'm no longer able

to hold up your world?

BEAN-NIGHE

You know the sort –
a pale little woman
who makes no mark on the world.
A woman you greet and then forget,
whose passing might sadden,
in the way of all passings,
but not for herself alone.

She's a sad little thing,
a widow, perhaps,
who lives her life
with a torn-eared cat,
and a patient collie,
at the far end of the bay
where the road dips down to the stream.

You see her sometimes
as the long day ebbs,
washing her sheets and petticoats,
in the pool below the ford.

And they say young Jock McLeod,
him that went off to the war,
saw her one evening,
as the gloaming caught in the gorse
and gilded the buttons
of the jacket he'd yearned to wear.

And they say, forby,
that he saw the sunset
run in the water like blood.

AM FEAR LIATH MÓR

Here, on the edge of things,
lies a different edge.
Up here on the grey heights,
in the wind's wail and the heather's rattle,
something is watching.

I am light, formless and fickle,
cloud, dropping like a stone,
rain, seaming the darkness,
ice, stitching the bone.
I am one step too far.

Tread carefully here, on the edge of things,
where the cloud is breaking, for I am waiting.
Here, in the crumble of granite,
you'll hear my footsteps
and taste my breath in your throat.

I am everything you've ever feared
and all you've ever wanted.
I am wilderness, turned in on itself,
a folding of the land by moonlight.
I am solitude, as empty as the wind,
a spectre, broken by the light.

I have no shape but the one you give me,
no name but the one you call me by.
I am not veiled, but am the veil itself.
Here, on the edge of things,
I am a different edge.

CARTOGRAPHIES

The ghosts are lifting from the land,
pale revenants bleached to a glimmer of bone.
They form at sunrise after snowfall in the night,
when the pitiless light of winter contours the past.
It shadows walls of fire-fused rock,
slants across squared ditches of occupation,
mounds itself in snail-coils of souterrains,
paints patterns on angled slabs of sandstone.

The ghosts rise out of the old stories –
cold kings and countless warriors,
soldiers and tribesmen withered by war.
They gleam with colour in the mist –
the red of a weathered cloak,
the blue of a woad-pricked design.
You can hear their voices in the wind,
an echo of nailed sandals,
the blare of a horn from the hills,
the stamp of a hoof in the woods.

The sun rises and shadows flatten
and ghosts vanish in the smoke of sublimation,
leaving little more than relics of their lives –
a rickle of bones in the fields,
the rust-fused blade of a knife,
a glint of gold in the turned soil.

But you can find them in the maps
we think are of the present,
in the names that mark
the borders of forgotten kingdoms,
in forts and duns and battlefields –
Stracathro, Catherun, Dunichen.
You can find them in their quiet graves,
these cartographies of ghost-fall.

ANCESTORS

The painted ones, a name
that is not your own,
inhabiting a land between
the known and the debatable worlds.

You left nothing on the tongue
but hints of structure
in the sound of places here and there –
Pittenweem, Pitscottie, Cardenden –
and little remains but king-lists,
shards of flint locked
behind smoked glass
smelling of camp fires,
and slabs of sandstone,
whorled and spiralled.

You lie uneasily
between bronze and iron,
anchored by stone
and the texts of those who fought against you.
You are sifted into all the folds
of stream and mere –
your bones and broken jars
beneath dunes or peat-dark waters,
your fragments of cloth
dyed with broom flowers
or the crushed ichor of shellfish.

All you left is gathered now
in chilled and empty spaces
of tungsten and glass
as dead as your tongue.
Yet you lie uneasily still
between blood and flesh,
anchored by our endless two-fold spirals.

Ancestral, known, disremembered.

HULK

She was sluggish at the end
when they hauled her
from her native element.
She'd had grace once,
the deep-bellied gravitas
of something old and canny.

Hers was the steady tidal drift,
the slow lift to each wave,
those heavy shoulders deep in foam.
Her voice was harsh:
the creak of cordage,
the crack of sailcloth,
and the taut shrouds singing.

But in time she grew old,
weed-foul and arthritic,
nail-sick in the quarter-knees,
teredo in the transom,
so they pensioned her off,
hauled her, gasping, from the sea,
and left her lying there, beached,
like a whale.

She complained at first.
She'd not yet lost her voice.
Her frayed rigging whined
and her timbers groaned
as she settled on the flats,
heavier now than on the billowed
breasting of the waves.

But in time she turned silent,
slipped into a doze that was half a dream
of coiling ink-black seas
beneath a firmament of night.

Her masts began to tilt,
a year-long rake against the sky,
and, gradually, she transformed herself
to ribs and spars and wooden bones
that one night slipped,
on tides swollen by a wash of rain,
down to the sea once more.

IDEAS

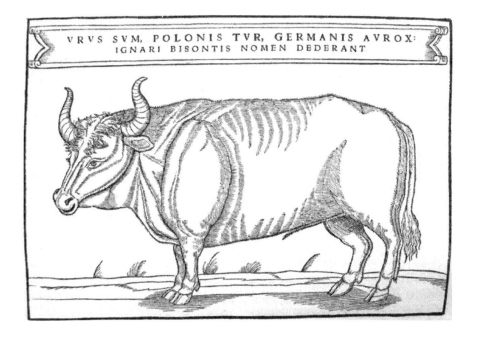

VRVS SVM, POLONIS TVR, GERMANIS AVROX:
IGNARI BISONTIS NOMEN DEDERANT

Now all that remains are smears
    of ochre
on a cave wall . . .

TAURUS

They will take the tooth of the beast
and find life in the dead bone.
They will unwind its essence
and tease from the tangled years
something stronger than rumour.
In that painless extraction
you can almost hear its roar.

Yet why not content ourselves with dumbness,
the placid chewing of the cud,
the ambling trail to the milking parlour,
the peaceful lowing of these moulded creatures?
The wildest beasts we know of now
are the black bulls of Catalonia,
and the horned and shaggy Highlanders.

But maybe we, in our Godless world,
search for a strength to confound our own.
Perhaps we long for the vanished ones –
Apis and Hathor of the Nile,
the slaughtered bull of Mithras,
the beasts who danced at Knossos
and ploughed the furrow of the sky.

Now all that remains are smears of ochre
on a cave wall, and the bones of beasts
four hundred years dead.
Yet they will take the teeth
from those vast skulls,
and goad these monstrous cattle
out of their myths – the Aurochs,
the Behemoth, the Minotaur.

ECLIPSE OF THE MOON

I'd expected it of course,
had known for weeks before,
had marked the date and time
and watched the forecasts.
18.42, they said,
if the skies are clear –
which they were that night.

And so I watched
for a confluence of spheres,
for light diffracting
according to the rules of optics –
Newtonian, exact, predetermined.

A miracle of physics,
or so they said, using tabloid words
for something not miraculous at all,
but a confirmation of all we knew,
of faith rooted deep in facts.

And yet when it began
it was none of these things,
no sharp-edged obfuscation,
no slide of wavelength,
but a gradual dimming from the south,
a strange necrotic cloud of night
that pulsed and blurred and deepened.

Then it was gone, the silver light –
that to my mind was fragile now,
beset by stars and the chills of space –
leaving in its place a colour
not red at all but ochre,
no portion of the spectrum
but something else, older than vision.

And so it seemed the moon I knew –
the serene and silver globe
that sails between the nebulae of space –
was now a bowl of blood, bleeding into a night
razor-sharp with stars.

No miracle this,
but an ancient horror.
No veiling of the light
but a stripping away.
A revelation of what we'd always feared –
the viral pulse of something mortal.

INADMISSIBLE EVIDENCE

We think we see things clearly now.
In spectral shifts we tease apart
the electronic arc of photons,
lay bare the spinning atom's heart.

We think we see things clearly now,
through lenses bent by silvered glass.
We've mapped the heaven in its vacuum,
resolved the stars to dust and gas.

So what is this that floats before us –
in darkened church, a drift of light,
a woman's form, a gleaming vessel,
a spear of rose that splits the night?

But no, it's just a trick of vision,
or else the heart that fools the mind.
There is no Grail, no call for questing.
We see things clear. We must be blind.

DOORWAY

In memory of Harry and Rambo, the best cats in the world.

In my house there is a door
that leads you nowhere now,
a relic of an unconverted time
before builders stripped away beams,
pulled down walls,
and opened up the loft to light.

But my cats remember,
insist on that door being opened –
the door that once led somewhere.
They think to find the dark ascent,
the windy space of joists and rafters,
chinks of light spearing the dust,
the musk-smell of mice
and fledglings under the eaves.

Sometimes, I too open a door
I think leads nowhere now,
and find instead a twisting stair –
the genome's coiling staggered tread.
It leads me backwards into the dark,
and I too creep on soft and careful feet,
wide-eyed in the wildness,
a huntress hunting down her past.

PRESENCE

You stand behind my right shoulder,
a sensed presence.
Yet you are silent, scentless, unreflecting,
and when my hand seeks yours
my finger close on absence.
My palm cups no more taste
than the salt of my own skin.

So are you angel or demon,
alien or god?
Or are you myself – alter ego, archetype,
the part that stands outside, weightless?
Sometimes I think you all the selves I never was,
the ghost of old dreams and faded hopes,
the shadow of the long defeat.

Perhaps I knew you better as a child,
when I gave you a name,
played with you in empty gardens,
insisted on a place being set at table.
Even now, in autumn, on the night of the dead,
I want to leave a space by the hearth.

But crowds disperse you.
Laughter shatters your illusion.
Sunlight drives you back –
although never entirely –
and when I'm alone in the dark,
or the cold, in the outer reaches of grief,
at the hard edges of the world,
you press closer than my own blood.

They have names for you there, in the empty places,
on the mountain heights, the arid deserts,
in the white-out of the poles.
They call you fetch, phantom, uraisg, yeti.
You are the good neighbour, Tanist, twin,
my own white lady.

Perhaps, in the end, when the last tide ebbs,
I will turn and greet you,
know you as angel and demon, alien and god,
know you as the other half of my soul.
Together, shoulder to shoulder,
we will walk towards the light.

ON GROWTH AND FORM

I hadn't thought of the crocodile as Cartesian.
It's more triangular in form,
with those sharp-toothed points,
that awkward angle of snapping jaw.

The square, however, has a homely feel,
a predictability of angles,
those equidistant sides of defined number,
co-ordinated and cubed.
Yet squares can change, apparently,
distort to quadrilaterals,
and we begin to feel unease,
sensing that beneath the surface
of this contorted grid
other crocodiles lie concealed –
other species from other continents
and other lines of evolution,
but still with jaws and teeth.

So take care when you look in mirrors.
Try not to see a grid of squares,
pixelated and precise,
for squares can shift and slide,
angles become acute, sides shorten,
and you may find yourself growing into the past.
Watch your arms lengthen,
your forehead shrink,
your body bend to touch the ground.

Or, worse than this, you might see,
within that shifting grid,
a shape you do not recognise –
a form moulded by an evolution still to come.

PHOTOSYNTHESIS

Once I had distance,
the blowing vastness of the wind,
but now you cling closer
than the clouds of my own breath.

I am the plane of the air,
you the rooted trees,
dressed in your fractals of bough and twig,
your suit of petalled leaves.

And in the summer light
you reach out to take part of myself.
You draw me into your green heart,
like the fly into the flower.

And there I am transformed,
my crabbed vapours changed -
an inspiration blooming into life.

ALTERED VISION

You get on the bus as usual,
but I see you differently these days
and you're no longer merely exotic.

Your skin is darker than mine,
your eyes more brilliant,
and I know now why you wear that veil –
to hide the hair that inflames desire
in my brothers and cousins.

But are we enemies, you and I –
or sisters under the skin,
with the same impatience of our faiths,
paying lip-service for convenience,
and standing by, embarrassed,
while they burn witches,

or infidels?

COCKEREL GENETICS

There's hierarchy in the farmyard,
a brash crowing from dung heaps,
a strutting and a showing off.
Here challenges are flung, hackles raised,
combs flaunted, vigour measured and compared.

Blazoned and plumed, their scales glint,
and frilled superfluous folds of flesh swell and tremble.
They are armed with spurs and slashing beak,
caparisoned in bronze and gold,
with mantlings of scarlet, as they enter the lists.

The rules are simple – winner takes all –
their prize the simpering gravid hens.
Eggs will be laid, chicks hatched,
genes dispersed, a proud lineage assured.

They could not know a modest monk
would cut them down to size,
explain the laws that rule their world
of posturing and display.
He labelled them with traits thought up in a moment –
foolish and demeaning.

For who can crow from dung heaps now,
knowing they bear the genes for *pea*
or *rose* or *walnut*?
It takes away their pride somehow,
their strutting sense of self,
their reason to crow at all.

Heraldry and hierarchy give way to science,
and Chanticleer concedes defeat
to the hierophant of genes.

INFRA-RED

We were hot, you and I,
warmed by love and wine -
burgundy and claret, and roses
as red as lipstick or lobsters.
You made me blush,
blood flaming into my face
with flames of gold and copper,
that turned to amber
when you gave me oranges,
and marmalade and honey,
topazed apricots and tangerines.
There were flowers too –
buttercups and daffodils,
primroses in sulphur and lemon.
Yet among them all was mustard
and brimstone for the yellow fever
that left you jaundiced and bilious,
and green with envy.

So then you brought me sourer fruit -
greengages, olives and limes.
You began to fade, like Lincoln Green
into the Greenwood, a gleam of jade
or emerald, a hint of aquamarine
from distant seas, as sapphire as the sky.

You were my blue-eyed boy,
in Air-force blue, or Oxbridge.
But I picked my own flowers then -
gentians and cornflowers,
forget-me-nots ironical in azure.
For you had turned cyanotic -
my sailor boy in navy, my ultramarine -
as blue as midnight on indigo nights
that sparkle with amethyst stars
and smell of heliotrope and lilac.

You leave me frigid now,
colder than a frozen violet.

Ultra-violet.

TO A COMPUTER

Crash! They put the boot in,
shattering my Windows
and littering the carpet with icons.
A password is no protection
against the boys in 32-bit colour.

One of them, bristling with hardware,
pulls out his sound-blaster,
and loads up his drivers.
'Freeze, you mother-boarder!' he yells
and double-clicks. So I run,
programs scrolling behind me,
to hide myself in an empty folder.
But their search engine finds me out,
drags me screaming to the desktop,
where I confess to the performance
of illegal operations in module 8096.

It's not my first offence.

Turns out they have a file on me,
downloaded from the Internet,
recording my failures to upgrade,
back up, log off.
I'm tried by a multimedia circus,
accused of incompatibility with printers,
a luddite tendency to DOS around,
the embezzlement of petty cache.

In my defence, I claim infection by a virus,
a temporary loss of memory,
but nothing can save my screen.
They find me guilty, read out the licence agreement,
ask for a final request – a last byte perhaps?

I'm locked up in an interface,
confined to a mouse-infested microchip,
not big enough to swing a cat in.
But I get parole for good behaviour,
release after a term of nanoseconds,
a reformatted character.

THE SPARE PAIR

I have bent light for you,
gathered it in from the fog,
laid it on veins and nerves.
We have made images together.

What worlds we've seen!
A dew drop on a spider's web,
a distant star netted in the moon,
the microcosm of a lover's skin,
all as sharp as a blade.

Where, then, did I go wrong?
Was mine a failure of diffraction, lucidity,
a subtle blur or haze?
Or was it that I saw too clearly?

My fault had less to do with seeing
than being seen.
You judged me too dull, too old-fashioned,
and grew tired of me.
So now you choose to see your world
through newer glassy eyes.

Now here I lie, discarded on a shelf,
my world drawn in to a plane of ceiling,
where motes of dust drift and settle
to cataract my sight.

ONE RED ROSE

One red rose, a conflagration of red,
scarlet, magenta, crimson and vermilion.
It fills my eye with blood,
my mind with thorns.

How should I describe such colour?
A rosy-cheeked maiden?
A poppy-bright sunset?
The ruby breast of a robin?

Slowly, by leaf and stem,
it grows in my mind,
takes shape word on word,
pruned and punctuated.
Each line is a drop of sweat,
a musk-scented dew
that fills my head with the smell of ink.

Black and white now,
a distillation of red,
my rose blooms on the page.
Quickly, while it's fresh,
I fold the sheet to seal its sweetness,
then stamp and send it.

Sometime, days from now,
you'll read my lines in black and white,
turn words into sounds,
hear my voice in your ear,
and see, perhaps, at the edge of your mind,
that first flush of rose.

Between seeing and believing

It was an odd thing to find in a modern plantation,
on a dull afternoon, a stone's throw from the track -
a little dwelling of twigs and moss and bracken

in an avenue of pines, hedged about by puzzles –
a sapling bent like a bow, five shells in a circle,
three jay's feathers hanging from a twig.

A drift of smoke rose as if from a smoored fire,
and there were sounds no bird could make –
the whistle of a bone flute, the tap of flint on stone.

I felt as if I'd walked miles to come there,
would walk further still to leave,
that I'd reached the white spaces on the chart.

The air hung like a cloak, and yet the light,
in that cathedral gloom of trees,
shivered as if a door had opened.

I moved to the dark mouth of the hut
expecting to find . . . what? Some tramp? A madman?
A shaman with his own religion?

But what I saw were bones –
the curved cage of ribs, the splayed limbs of a sacrifice,
white with age, picked clean of flesh.

Afterwards, I said that the world stopped.
In truth it went on beating away,
but it was no longer the same world.

In that moment, between seeing and believing,
tectonic plates shifted and light altered.
The earth hummed and creaked as if that door,

opening, had closed once more. A threshold loomed
and I, unknowing, crossed over. There were no givens here,
no proven theorems, no surety, no safety.

In this world anything was possible;
ghosts and goblins, unicorns, night parrots,
dogs with eyes as big as tea-cups. Gods.

And then the moment was gone. I'd seen and believed,
but now I understood. Those bones were branches of pine
bleached by the sun, this place a trick of the light.

There was no shaman, no truths but the ones I knew.
I walked to the track, a stone's throw away,
and never went back. But I still remember

that moment, between seeing and believing,
when certainty shimmered and dissolved and congealed.
I think of everything I clung to. And everything I lost.

GODS

We thought that we were safe,
that you were confined by distance
or disbelief, hidden in an oak grove
or the bole of a willow,
ringed by stone or buried beneath,
chained beyond the horizon,
imprisoned in the infinity of space.

We thought you were diminished,
a question of debate or definition,
restricted by the written word,
the discourses of men wiser
than we believed ourselves to be.

We laid you beneath spires,
on altars, in a maze of incense,
in empty spaces of wood and glass.
You were thorned and nailed in alcoves,
chained in gold about our necks.

We delved deep in the earth
for lack of evidence,
searched within the hiss of space
for silence.

And then we closed the book,
found other faiths – theorems, hypotheses,
economies of thought –
and considered we were safe.

Yet here we dwell in voided space,
in choired silence, in vacant time,
in vacuums of our own construction
that Gods rush in to fill.

THE HUMAN CONDITION

Soon, a phrase from now,
you'll be grace and form
and weightless.

CORPS DE BALLET

Half-lit by limelight,
you're watching patiently.
Poised, you wait your turn,
listening to the music,
the glide and sweep,
the shifts of key.
You feel its pull.

Soon, a phrase from now,
you'll all move to the same tide.
Together, you will slowly bend,
each arm curved to shape itself
in a reflection of the next.
Arcs will be inscribed,
planes of space made flesh.
Then, a moment's balance
and a falling away,
a white wave coiling to the shore,
an arabesque of silk
on the fading breath of a nocturne.

Soon, a phrase from now,
you'll be grace and form
and weightless.

But for now you're watching patiently.
Poised, you wait your turn,
half-lit by limelight.

WILLOW PATTERN

I take one of our precious plates –
the ones with the willow pattern –
and hold it tenderly with fingers
that have stroked your hair.

I feel the heft of it in a hand
that has held yours on summer evenings.
I search for my life in the tale of the plate –
the girl with the bound feet, the poet lover.

Would you scale walls for me? Brave
the raging torrent? Would you steal me away?
Would I, like her, die in a fire for you?
I take one of our precious plates,

the ones with the willow pattern.
It tells a story other than our own.
So I take the plate with its tale of love,
and gently let it fall.

LOVE SHOULD BE LIGHT

Love should be light, they say,
a breath of air on the throat,
a trace of moisture at lip or eye,
a dissolving sweetness on the skin –
insubstantial and instantly forgotten.

Not this weight, this gravitas,
this dull resentment of a force
that draws my lodestone to your north.

I am leaden with your minutiae,
the cadence of your voice,
the turn of your head,
a glance that's held but drifts away.

My eyes are earthed by your geographies,
your contours and shadings,
your landscapes unexplored,
the white spaces on your chart.

You are the world, and I the air,
love the gravity that holds me fast,
leaving you unchanged,
centred in your core of self.

I am no moon to swell your tides
but the air itself,
drawn down from the stars,
light and insubstantial.

AS

As the candle's flame
gathers the moths,
so I am drawn to you.

As the compass blade
pulls to the north,
so I turn in your direction.

As the noon-day sun
tilts the sunflower's face,
so I gaze on your face.

As the rising moon
laps at the river's mouth,
so I kiss your cold white cheek.

As the falling stream
breaks on the rocks,
so am I broken, broken, broken.

DREAM

The miracle of transformation –
man becomes wolf,
woman becomes swan.

I watched the wolf lope north,
head for winter-mantled mountains,
while I, dark-feathered,
beat the wind with my wings.

I tried to follow, to soar, to glide,
to wing my way through the chill of crystal.
I longed to lose myself
in eyes the colour of a storm.

But storms edge themselves away,
dwindle to a growl of thunder,
and a swan grows weary of the flight.

Waking, I recalled the tethers
that bind me to the earth -
family, country, duty, need.

Love.

GOLD

I just wanted to look,
to let the brightness of you
break through my dark.
I wanted to print you
on the back of my eyes,
lay you down in the meadow
of my retina and make love
to you there, unnoticed.

I didn't want to touch,
to make you bear the weight
of my regard. I didn't want
to change you, to dull your glow
as wind cools the molten gold.

I wanted nothing from you
but the fact of you in the world,
immutable.
Instead, I find the world itself
has changed, and me within it.

Time passes, and you, unnoticing,
pass with it, like a liner in the fog.
You are one last gleam of sun,
one burst of gold in the east,
one endless longing
that will never leave me.

ONCE

Once, returning home on the slow train,
mid-week, mid-afternoon, mid-December,
we stopped, unaccountably,
on the bridge.

Suddenly, there was silence –
no click-clack of track,
no gusting sigh of engine,
just the slow ticking of the world.

All at once, I understood
how things are centred, as I was then –
poised above a river
edging to the flood, stationary
between two kingdoms,
the sun setting behind hills,
the moon rising above dunes.

I seemed to be held in a network of steel,
no less strong, or weak,
than the web of the familiar.
Sitting there, on the bridge,
I was drawn by those two spheres,
those two places, as the tide is pulled,
lured both by home and the unknown.

And I knew it would always be like this –
trying to return,
but never quite arriving.

LIVING IN THE MOMENT

There have been times
when I've looked forward,
imagining the day
when I'd be other than I am –
calm, poised and in control.
My talents would be recognised,
my life examined
and found to be complete.

Yet I know a time will come
when I'll look back,
be prone to starting conversations
with *when I was young,* or *in my day.*
I'll grow regretful, nostalgic for a time gone by.

But, in the moment, I find myself
poised, as I'd always hoped to be.
Finally, I seem to be in balance,
having reached the apogee
in the long arc of desire.
And, here on the heights,
I see things clearly,
not forwards or back,
no dizzy vertigo of down,
but simply now, minutely.

I see the angle of a seagull's wing,
the perfect green of a leaf.
I feel the warmth of a man's sleeping body.

Not then, but now.
Not that, but this,
and this and this,

and this.

NOCTURNE I

Slip inside your own head.
Slide beneath today's events,
tomorrow's fears. Spiral inwards.
Here are worlds beyond time,
transient, eternal. Sound shifts
to smell, touch to vision.

Stand on the edge of this cliff
and let yourself fall upwards.
There are no dimensions here, or many,
no language you can't understand,
no music you can't wrap yourself around.

Become nothing more than pulses of light,
spikes of frequency caught up
in a network of nerves.

Sleep, they say, is the little death
you practice nightly until, one day,
you get it right.

NOCTURNE II

We ought to fear the dark,
its gathering, the way it creeps
out of the corners.
We ought to fear the fall
in temperature, the cold calling
of night birds.

There are no certainties at dusk,
no promises to rely upon.
Every evening could be an ending,
each encroaching dark the death
of everything we know.

And yet we seem to welcome
the daily blurring of the edges.
We draw closer to the fire, to each other.
We wrap ourselves in blankets,
in warm familiar flesh.

In time we'll sleep and dream
of a sun rising in a clear sky.
Each night our given task
is to dream ourselves back into the day.

FOUND

To dig in the garden is to go back in time.
I find the roots of long-dead shrubs,
stones from an old path,
pegs from a washing line,
shards of glass and patterned china.
Then something I can't quite place –
a pierced and polished disc of stone.

It could have been a counter
in a child's game, the pendant of a priest,
a housewife's spindle weight.
Was it lost by chance, or buried by design?
Was it secret, symbol, offering?

I think of all the things I have lost
and wonder if they too will be found.
Will some spade turn over my hopes?
Or find, beneath a layer of sand, my youth?
Will they unearth some artefact
they won't recognise as me?

LEARNING TO SWIM

(after Stevie Smith)

Thrown in at the deep end,
I'm required to sink or swim,
and my body chooses to sink.
But my limbs rebel –
legs thrashing the water,
arms threshing the air –
as I go down for the third time.
Not swimming but sinking.
Not waving but drowning.

But in the sea it's different,
in the saline surge of the waves,
the lift and buffet of tumbled water,
in the cool clasp of a tilting meniscus.
Surprised, I find myself buoyant,
bobbing, drifting, floating.
See how far out I am now!
Not sinking but swimming.
Not drowning but waving.

LEAVING

For Eileen.

Do you hear the sound of an unanswered phone,
the hum of a screen left blank?
That is the sound of a willed silence.
Listen, then, to each moment,
unmarred by anything of need,
each hour, unlimited.

Hold it in the palm of your hand
and see its transformation
to music or verse, the sweet turnings of language,
to brushstrokes or dance-steps.
It flexes with possibility.

Hold fast to that thought, or let it slip.
Cast forth on a journey, or remain,
tethered by the holdfast of home.
Come and go as you please,
for all things can happen now.

So let it unfold softly,
or swiftly as you choose.
Take the high road or the low,
the wrong side of the tracks.
Leave the lanes untraveled.

Take the bit between your teeth,
the law into your own hands.
Wear cerise or lime-green,
dye your hair purple.
Care for no opinion but your own.

This is *your* time now.

PHOTOGRAPHER

He takes aim and fires
then holds light hostage,
chained in silver,
blindfolded in a million cells.
An expression is snatched
and held to ransom,
a cry of protest stilled.

He takes every moving moment,
binds it to an endless present,
and leaves us, in the end,
with nothing but exposures of our past –
lives pressed between pages,
blurred memories in sepia.

So perhaps we all should face his lens
with our eyes wide open –
unsmiling, ready for the shot,
the white magnesium flare –
aware he'll take us captive,
and that he'll steal our souls.

DARK SIDE OF THE MOON

I'm waiting for my name to be called,
in a room with other women,
while outside, in a winter sky,
a half-moon rises.

Two weeks ago it was a crescent,
a skim of light on a shadowed globe.
Two weeks ago I didn't know
about the moon.

But now I've traced its surface
as if it's my own skin,
and know the names of craters,
seas of dust, the pock-marks of meteorites,
for I have seen the moon in a new light,
imaged by X-rays and ultra-sound.

So now I wait for my name to be called,
wait for a part of me, not mapped before,
to be recognised and termed.
Is it a crater filled with fluid,
or a spreading sea of cells?

I'm waiting for my name to be called,
in a room with other women,
astronomers against our wills,
familiar with what we now know lies
on the dark side of the moon.

TEETH

In memory of my late father

He used to have his own teeth.
white and strong and functional,
so he took them for granted.

But times change. Gums recede
like the tide. A man's years
recede like the tide. He began
to lose his grip on everything
that mattered. First the hair,
then the knee joints,
then the strength in his hands.

The teeth were only one such
abandonment, only the first
of the holes he came to live with.

When I think of him now
I remember those gaps in his smile,
and tongue the space he left in my own.

In memoriam

So, it's like this –
the sweetest shot,
the high flat curve of it,
flighting into the sun.

It's the way the wind
takes hold to arc and turn,
until you're blinded
by its brilliance.

It's the way the heart
grows great to hold
its freight of years
and moments.

It's the way a life
drives home,
straight down the fairway,
true and free,
and perfect.

FAIRWAY

This is the last buoy.
The Fairway, it is called,
but from this place I fear
the way will not be fair,
for little lies between
these grey-green damasked waters
and impossible depths,
but things that are not seals,
or weed, or anything else
known or imagined.

This is the last buoy.
Remember how it was we came?
We slipped our moorings on a falling tide,
caught our own drift,
then named each passing point –
the Craig, the Pool, the Abertay.
We altered our bearings,
judged direction and distance,
speed over the ground,
and dead-reckoned our way

to this, the last buoy.
Tip-tilted on its tether
it semaphores blindly,
rocking itself to silence.
Yet shouldn't there be music here,
the clang of a bell, a breathy whistle,
the wolf-howl of a horn,
rhythms to grace the snare-drum of each swell?

Instead we hear a different song –
the sail-slap in the shrouds,
a shackle's rattle,
the fading shudder of the luff.

This is the last buoy,
a notch in the knife blade of sky,
in the rim of the world,
at the land's last holding.
Wind fades, then tide,
and we drift together for a while,
as if we too are held by chains,
rusting and mortal,
to this place of gathering in

or casting loose.

JOURNEY, INTERRUPTED

He has fallen asleep,
lulled by the purr of diesel,
the hypnosis of fields
freeze-framing his window.
Power-lines snake by; roads converge.
Tunnels blare briefly into black.

It takes a hush of brakes to wake him,
the slow slide to stasis.
There's rain on his window,
beyond, a long grey platform.
But isn't this the through-train?
Wasn't the sky clear of clouds?

This station has no buildings, no name.
No door opens on a hiss.
No-one gets off or on
to push past sleeping travellers.
He is the only one awake.
So, should he gather his bags?
Should he alight?

Too late, the platform starts to slide away,
becomes a motion blur of grey,
a rain-smeared rear-view vision.
Fields reform, telegraph lines converge
at infinity. He rushes over the horizon.

One day he'll retrace this journey.
A long white tunnel will lead him
to this platform once more.
He will leave his possessions behind.
He will alight into the unknown.

NOTES

*Appeared in 'The Dark Side of the Moon' published in 2010

The ghost in the machine (page 1) is a term coined by British philosopher Gilbert Ryle to describe the dualism of Descartes, which considers that the human body is a machine and only becomes a 'person' when infused with an immaterial soul. Written in 2006.

Archaeopteryx (page 7) is the earliest bird known. They lived during the late Jurassic period, about 150-145 million years ago. Written in 2003.

Owl (page 8) was written in 2017.

Peregrine (page 9) This poem was written in response to *The Bridges of Madison County* but Robert James Waller. The poetic form used is iambic pentameters. Written in 2009.

Oystercatchers (page 10) The financial crash of 2008 resulted in some investment bankers allegedly being unable to afford champagne and oysters. Written in 2017

Hawking (page 11) was written in response to a weekend of hawking with some Harris Hawks. We caught one hare. Written in 2003.

Brock (page 12) is a 50 word poem, written in 2017.

Horses (page 13) was one of several poems written in response to the first line of another poem. Written in 2006.

Notes (continued)

Snowdrops (page 14) was written in 2011.

Woolly willow (page 15) is a sub-arctic species of willow found at high altitude in a few places in the Scottish Highlands. Written in 2017.

*Winter I (page 16) was written in 2001

Winter II (page 17) was written in 2017

*Temperature inversion (page 18) results in colder air and fog in mountain valleys, while summits can be warm and sunny. Written in 2006.

Summers (page 20) was written in response to childhood memories of summer holidays. Written in 2001.

*November, (page 23), originally entitled 'Bonfire', was written in 2003.

Low springs (page 24) was written in 2017.

*Ben Nevis (page 25) was written in 2001.

Climbing the line (page 26) was written in response to a rock-climbing course I went on. Written in 2013.

Rounding the Horn (page 36) makes reference to the tea-clipper trade. Written in 2017.

Munro-bagging (page 28) involves climbing all hills in Scotland over 3000 ft, of which there are currently 282. Written in 2001.

Forest (page 29) is one of number of poems about a piece of woodland we own. Written in 2017.

*Moorland in rain (page 30) was written in response to the first line of another poem, in this case by Alun Lewis. Written in 2006

Notes (continued)

Island I (page 31) was written in response to the first line of a poem by Ian Crichton Smith. Written in 2010.

Island II (page 32) was written in response to the island of Mull. Written in 2002.

River (page 34) was written in 2017.

Daedalus (page 39) was the father of Icarus, who fell to earth after the wings his father had made melted when he flew too close to the sun. Written in 2006.

Orb-weaver (page 40) is one of the common web-spinning spiders. Clotho, Lachesis and Atropos are the three Fates, who spin, measure and cut the thread of life. Written in 2013.

Dryad (page 41) is the spirit of a tree in Greek mythology. Written in 2017.

Waiting for Ragnarok (page 42) was written in response to a local weathervane in the shape of a wyvern, a winged variety of dragon. Ragnarok, in Norse mythology, is a great battle foretold to result in the death of the Gods.

Yggdrasil (page 44) in Norse mythology, is the ash-tree that holds up the world. The poem makes reference to the disease of ash die-back. Written in 2013.

Bean-nighe (page 45) is Gaelic for 'the washer woman', a fairy who washes the blood from the grave-clothes of those about to die. Written in 2002.

Am in *Fear Liath Mór* (page 46) is Gaelic for The Big Grey Man, a presence or creature said to haunt the summit and passes of Ben Macdui in the Cairngorms. Written 2006.

Notes (continued)

Cartographies (page 48) was written in response to the Picts, one of the ancient peoples of Scotland. Written in 2010.

*Ancestors (page 50) was also written in response to the Picts. Written in 2000.

*Hulk (page 52) was written in 2001

*Taurus (page 57) was written in response to 'Project Taurus', a consortium of scientists using DNA extracted from the teeth of extinct aurochs to steer a breeding programme designed to 'recreate' these giant cattle. Written in 2010.

*Eclipse of the moon (page 58) was written in response to a lunar eclipse in 2001. Written in 2001.

*Inadmissible evidence (page 60) is one of my rare rhyming poems. Written in 2003.

*Doorway (page 61) was written in response to my cats' disappointment over a loft conversion. Written in 2003.

*Presence (page 62) refers to the 'sensed presence', experienced in extreme conditions, the conviction that someone else is there. Written in 2010.

*On Growth and Form (page 64) is the title of a seminal work on evolution by D'Arcy Thompson, written in 1915. Thompson explored the degree to which differences in form could be described by mathematical transformations of grid co-ordinates.

Photosynthesis (page 66) was written in 2010.

*Altered vision (page 98) was written in 2002.

NOTES (CONTINUED)

Cockerel genetics (page 68) was written in response to a museum exhibit demonstrating the genetics of comb formation in chickens. 'Rose', 'Pea' and 'Walnut' are different forms of the comb. Mendel, a 19th century Austrian monk, is famous as the originator of the science of genetics. Written in 2001.

Infra-red (page 70) was written in 2001.

To a computer (page 72) is the oldest poem in this collection, as evidenced by the references to outdated computer technology. Written in 1998.

The spare pair (page 74) was written in 2004.

One Red rose (page 75) is a poem about writing poetry. We've all done it. Written in 1998.

Between seeing and believing (page 76) was written in response to an otherworldly experience in a local forest. Written in 2017.

Gods (page 78) was written in 2000.

Corps de ballet (page 83) was written in 2005.

Willow pattern (page 84) was written in response to the first line of another poem. Written in 2006.

Love should be light (page 85) was written in 2000.

As (page 86) was written in 2006.

Dream (page 87) explores elements of one of my forthcoming historical novels, *The Swan in Summer.* Written in 2020.

Notes (continued)

Gold (page 88) was written in 2010.

Once (page 89) was written in response to a journey across the rail bridge over the River Tay. Written in 2005.

Living in the moment (page 90) was written in 2004.

Nocturne I (page 92) was written in 2017

Nocturne II (page 93) was written in 2017

Found (page 94) was written in 2017.

Learning to swim (page 95) was written in response to Stevie Smith's poem 'Not Waving, but Drowning'. Written in 2013.

Leaving (page 96) was written in honour of a friend and colleague who was retiring. Written in 2010.

Overheard conversation (page 99) was written in 2017.

Photographer (page 100) was written in 2005.

Dark side of the moon (page 101) was written in 2004.

Teeth (page 102) was written in memory of my late father. Written in 2017.

In memorium (page 103) was written in response to the death of a relative, a keen golfer. Written in 2005.

Fairway (page 104) is a navigation buoy in the River Tay, as are the Craig, Pool and Abertay buoys. Written in 2005.

Journey, interrupted (page 105) is another poem about death. Written in 2017.

Notes (continued)

In addition to appearing in 'The Dark Side of the Moon', as indicated, some of the poems in this collection, or earlier versions, have appeared in the following exhibitions or publications.

On Growth and Form and *Cockerel genetics* – A Private View (exhibition) (2001).

Winter I and *Eclipse of the moon* – Afterimage (2002).

Ancestors and *Gods* – Riverrun (2003).

Altered vision and *Hawking* – Contact, University of Dundee (2003 and 2004)

Corps de ballet, Hulk and *Photographer* – Timelines (2005)

Love should be light, Willow pattern, Moorland in rain and *As* –Sunrise over Machu Picchu (2010)

Oystercatchers – The Open Mouse (2017)

A number of poems were the inspiration for short stories that appear in my short story collection *The Man who Loved Landscape and other stories*. (See following page for details.) These include *Am Fear Liath Mór, Photographer* and *Fairway*.

ABOUT THE AUTHOR

I was born, and still live, in Scotland on the shores of a river, between the mountains and the sea. I'm a retired scientist and science administrator, but have always been fascinated by the early history of Scotland, and I love fleshing out that history with the stories of fictional, and not-so-fictional, characters.

I've had a number of short stories published in various anthologies and magazines and, in *The Man who Loved Landscape*, published in 2020, I've gathered together some of my favourites. Many of them are set in Scotland.

To find out more about this collection, visit: getbook.at/Manwholovedlandscape or scan this code:

A longer historical short story, *Song of a Red Morning,* which takes place in 6th century Scotland, was published in 2019.

To find out more about this story, visit: getbook.at/Songofaredmorning or scan this code:

Song of a Red Morning is set at Dunpeldyr, the Iron Age Fort of Traprain Law in East Lothian. This is also one of the settings for my Dark-age Trilogy, *The Trystan Trilogy*, which consists of *The Wolf in Winter, The Swan in Summer* and *The Serpent in Spring*. *The Wolf in Winter* will shortly be published in e-book and paperback form.

Find out more about me and my writing on my website:

Barbaralennox.com

Connect with me on the following:

Twitter   twitter.com/barbaralennox4
Instagram   instagram.com/barbaralennoxwriter
Goodreads   goodreads.com/author/show/19661962.Barbara_Lennox
Pinterest   pinterest.co.uk/barbaralennox58
Amazon   viewauthor.at/authorprofile

ACKNOWLEDGEMENTS

I would never have written any of these poems if I hadn't attended the 'Continuing as a Writer' classes, part of the University of Dundee's Continuing Education Programme. These classes were tutored by Esther Read whose support and encouragement has been unstinting and invaluable. Esther, I can't thank you enough. I'm also grateful to the other members of the class, and the Nethergate Writers Group, for their helpful and constructive criticism. I also owe a debt to the late Dr Jim Stewart, poet and inspirational teacher, who took the time to read through and give advice on many of these poems.

At home, Harry, Rambo and Oscar, the best cats in the world, were with me all the way, usually asleep.

Finally, but not least, I'd like to thank my husband, Will, for putting up with all this poetry.

Internal image attributions (first three sourced from Wikipedia)

Page 5: Eleventh Archaeopteryx specimen, Senckenberg Museum, Frankfurt, Germany. (CC BY 2.0) Allie Caulfield
Page 37: Fall of Icarus, 17th century relief, Musée Antoine Vivenel, Compiegne, France. (Public Domain) WMPearl
Page 55: Illustration of an Auroch from a book published in 1556, by Sigismund von Herberstein. (Public Domain)
Page 81: Photograph of dancers by Evgen Rom, made available through Pixabay.com

Printed in Great Britain
by Amazon